Talk Like Galileo

DAVID SERGEANT

Talk Like Galileo

Shearsman Books
Exeter

Published in the United Kingdom in 2010 by
Shearsman Books Ltd
58 Velwell Road
Exeter EX4 4LD

ISBN 978-1-84861-112-2
First Edition

Acknowledgements
See page 73.

CONTENTS

Process	11
The Cornish Chough	12
In Spring	15
Cooking Up	16
Epitaph for a Footballer	17
One and the Other	18
Out Past Tregonebris	20
Tiger Visitation	22
Fronting Out	23
Guy Fawkes Night	24
The Forest	26
The Wound	28
A Breach	29
Night Out	30
What You Eat	33
The Two Ages of a Footballer	36
Identifying Trees	37
Sparrows	39
O I Love You	40
Conversation	42
The Drum	43
Three Love Sonnets	44
A Kind of Love	47
Chaos River Section	48
The Summoning	49
Autumn-Time	50
Waking Midwinter	51
'Can I Create Here . . .'	52
This Civilisation	53
Lift Off	55
Levi	56
From the Sea Fields	57
21st Century West	58

His Grip   59
Poem for a Country Pub   60
Adam's Curse   61
Playing   63
Relationship in Two Parts   64
Co-ordinates   66
'Beautiful, we barged . . .'   67
Phwoar   68
Meadow Lane   69

Acknowledgements   73

Talk Like Galileo

for my Mum and Dad

Process

To gain this, gain this element
Bangled as a leopard skin with shapes itself

Which might be hung up like a curtain to dry
But would fructify into a crystal surface

Through which you'd see what was, what was not there
(Presence coding through the beads of air)

People off moving at an incredible distance
Smoke uprising from astounded chimneys

On which you know you'd cut yourself if you were there
So sharp they seem, malignant,

Like the brother of a man you might have killed
The ink you spilled so many years ago

Uprising now, its fingers round your neck
(Each cause regathered by its lost effect)

And everyone agrees the noose's fist
A monkey's hand that's shrivelled to a grip

Completes your look, as when a necktie shifts
And seals the knot above the spotless breast.

The Cornish Chough

*The chough has long been associated with Cornwall but has been
extinct there for several decades. There have recently been attempts to
reintroduce it into the county.*

Well, I've seen them too. Have seen, in fact, two,
Or even three
Of the famous birds. The first out near Land's End:
A man beside a dog accosted me
In a most unusual way, and pointing through
A drifting fume of cliff-side seasonal mist,
He sectioned out what seemed to be a crow
And expanse of granite, and patting his
Binoculars invoked the RSPB
And whispered chough. '*Chough.*'

Pronounced to rhyme with 'muff' or 'duff' or 'rough.'
A word my friends
And I had used, with more phonetic spelling,
To signify the touch that might attend
To one's own knob, in the argot of our youth.
Not to be found in any extant dictionary—
Trans. and intrans. verb, you know, *to chuff.*
He was dialling the Royal Society
As I looked back from the pathway's trailing end
And then departed

Into another season, climbing toward
The meadowed peaks
That rise above Nanjulian, the land
A glossy heft and wend of streaks,
The grass-blades ceding, mixing, straining forward.
There I saw two I knew, strutty old crows,
But with a jolly sailor's gait that led

To that programmatic jump where you just know
You already know something: their curvy beaks
A flippant red

And the cry all wrong, a kind of zapping bled
Through distortion
With a comic fall at the end. *Choughs*, I thought,
And squinted to enjoy them through the sun—
Thought of calling a friend but thought instead
Of the pamphlets and anthologies I'd seen
Who'd welcome a bastard sort of Keatsian ode
On a Celtic-cultural resurrection theme,
The soul come home, the exile seen in vision,
A blanker slate

The uninvited centuries vacate
To leave a place
Where spirit stands untrammelled. Harmless, no?
I watched them pick across the threshy space,
Cawing to each other. Another date,
Another country . . . and can you see them then,
Wee little Balkan beasties, picking at
The faultlessly ethnic brain
Of a Serb or Croat? Branding-marks of race,
Of tendered soil

And all that virtue. Of course, it's laughable:
Not here, not now,
And not with this, a dim romantic crow
Convenient for those who'd like to go
And live on cliffs apart from other people.
But still, an epigram: beware the one
Who'd take a definition like a pill

Or nail the breeding wind against your tongue.
Beware the country singular as snow.
I thought of one,

Lover of poetry, gentle Yorkshireman,
His words to me:
'The most Cornish person I ever knew
Was French: she'd dive each day into the sea,
Come rain, come shine, through every bloody season.
Now pass me that through your *identity*.'
O femme aquatic! I'd eulogise that run,
That plunge, to self-located buoyancy
But look—the choughs are readying to fly.
Regard the rock-

ing on the feet, the mutual crouch and set,
The final cawing.
From here they'll go the trackless coastal way
And let the currents justify the wing
On which they ride—a current I might take
Myself, upon the edge, approaching here,
An ocean breath to mix-in and translate.
Perhaps you feel it now upon your ear—
The softest kiss, that faint withdrawing
Waking note?

In Spring

The bony trees
Fork into the sky like tributaries—
I had forgotten.

There, and then here.
The blossom
Is clouds of pink bees

Or confetti, entranced.
If I were tiny
I'd clamber through

And open each bud like a letter.
How the jeans you wear
Unzip

Cooking Up

Mmm-mmm, sweet chicken glazed in honey,
Kinda sexual. Now take these lines of coke
And snort them off the face of this steel knife
And smack the open face of this steel pan
Because the steroids we've been taking in the changing room
Are peck-peck-peckering away
Like every cock is turned into a finger
Tapping on a door, or perhaps vice-versa,
Never-mind, I SAID CHOP—

Reduce your chicken stock and stall in jus;
Rabbit meat is underrated;
I source my produce loose from farms of puce;
My biceps are richer than Braille
Beneath the fingers of a blind woman
And with my cooked spaghetti
I could tie your spindle arms behind your back
And fuck you on the counter from behind
Till you gagged.

Did I just say that? Never-mind. I need a haircut.
WAITER! In this quintessence
Of essence of excellence
You see an image of the Holy Virgin
Done out in tarragon and butter
With nipples of cream. WAITER!
I own a house, a farm, a house in London,
Another house, a farm, and a nuclear shelter.
WAITER! My quads are those of a boxer:
I will go down fighting.

Epitaph for a Footballer

So blessed, he spoke no language people speak
When visiting the Queen or on the street,
But spoke the language of his twinkling feet.

Each game's a perfect sentence never heard
And players grope to find a single word:
He lived inside each sentence till it stirred.

But off the pitch he could not get it right,
Like trying to walk by using laws of flight
And make the difference up with booze each night.

Picture in his prime the crowds he drew,
The games that ebbed and flew, his give and glide.
What would it take to understand each pass?
He got slotted through
The gates of life, was waved onside
And is now beyond us.

One and the Other

I

So you're on me and I'm in you—
Speaking metaphysically of course—
And who I am is what you do
And every touch comes double back with force—

II

And every touch comes double-backed.
I pull my hips, hard-down, against my hips
And feel the gorge of what I lacked:
I feel the imprint of my fingertips.

III

Until, ta-da, you've vanished!
And I am left alone upon the bed
Half-conscious that, inflamed and famished,
I've bolted down your eyes, your heart, your head;

IV

Half-conscious that, yoghurt in milk,
I've spread my culture, transferred *yours* to *mine*;
Have pushed the knife in to the hilt
Until the knife is all that I can find.

V

My lust becomes my love, my love,
It bodies out the thing it wants to meet:
My dreams will clothe you like a glove:
A lonely spider rocks itself to sleep.

Out Past Tregonebris

His name was Berry Something and he lived
Out past Tregonebris, near Lamorna.
He walked the cliffs
On evenings and weekends, vetch and thrift
Were company for him, and the sea's far
Glitter and uncoil. He lived,

As I might have said, alone, drank pints with mates,
And had an office job and on-off girlfriend.
Later he'd sit
Not twiddling his thumbs but seemingly gripped
By the inletting and contours of his hands:
A puzzle you'd create

Then solve, then break and try to solve again.
That was later, years, after he'd begun
To drop each day
To what I'd call the littoral zone, that splay
Of tumbled granite, hanging grass, that hung
Beneath the cliff-path's rim,

Beyond the walker's limits, and ended
Where the contact happens, rock and ocean.
He didn't talk
Exactly of this but not being balked
By oddness I would sit and slowly begin
To glimpse or understand

The in-swell of the cauldron-spilling mix
Of turquoise through the deepness near the shore,
Beneath the surface,
Where the stones with every wave displace

Their dimple image and seemingly pour
A little forward, then fix

With the wave's back-swell or passing, into place.
Or rooks, you know, would sit and seem like friends.
Days he'd spend
Like this, till every working day would end
With those descents, like a man with the bends
Going deeper to escape

That sizzle in the blood, the rock and tilt
Of traffic and pollution in the head.
Better the sun
Crinkling the ocean every dawn.
His main emotion was fear, he said:
Guilt, and fear, and guilt.

Tiger Visitation

The living room was blue enchanted ice;
It felt like Christmases from long ago;
You might pick up that room and shake it twice
And feel your eyelids bat against the snow.

The visitor was perched in grandpa's chair;
The tiger sprawled along the furthest wall;
We watched it with polite uncertain stares,
Its shoulders drooped, its head between its paws—

Its head a block which yielded to your touch,
Your hands which pressed into its blazing fur,
Like pushing through a rabbit's baking hutch
Or grass in which you feel the country stir—

'We've found,' he said, the man in grandpa's chair,
Leant forward and with tears inside his throat,
'We've found,' he said, 'the scientists declare—'
His fingers twitching, desperate for a smoke—

'We've found that animals whose young we hunt,
That something happens to their vocal cords—
Their voice, it changes, gets a special note—
We've got no doubt—have heard it—made records—'

The tiger lay not moving on the floor,
A statuary block all streaked with paint,
Its eyes were closed, you could not see it stir—
Perhaps its breathing, soft, like snow, and faint.

Fronting Out

        to the storm's upcoming bar of purple—
Listen people!
        —I lower my head and shoulder on
To where the grass threshes and glows a lime-green
In alarm, signaling to itself, to anyone
The storm that is coming.
                I hunch and continue,
Mad with the energy crackle.
          The trees are going mental, loving it,
        Balloons of panic
Lurching against their shackles, shoals of ripped-up paper
   Dropped and held
          In forking hands

  From which the wind flees
            And depresses,
Dropping onto the river
   Where it whips up and rides
Little arrow-shaped horses
       In fan-wide dispersals of panic,
An army retreating over and over again
The same old ground, from second to second.

Thunder booms and rolls itself
Out of bed: the air smells of rain
And wet tin.
      The storm is coming.
           Listening to it.

Guy Fawkes Night

Sweetheart, they lined the street: the whites, browns, blacks,
The browns and blacks, the whites, the rich and poor,
Christian, Muslim, whatever, they stood together,
And fireworks were what they stood there for.

Each face upturned, each group outside its house.
I went by every one—well, you know me—
And went unseen, they did not watch each other,
But parents knelt by children so they'd see

Each blast above the park, each rain of fire,
They pointed each one down, watched each one burn . . .
You know these people, see them every day,
Familiars from our makeshift segregation,

But separate—not like this, where each is joined
But separate, like the contents of a census,
Or sacks laid round to anchor the balloon
As it swells into the sky and starts to rise

And goes into the ropes and ropes them tight,
The sky itself flung off, replaced by burning . . .
Later I went into the park—a crowd—a fire—
A pile of crates as massive as a building

But weeping off itself in walls of flame
That were not walls, but flashed rehearsals,
An image of itself that came again,
And again, and again, as if it might, was hopeful

That one day it would come right. I left
Before it could crumble into slush.

Its heat was still on my face when I came here,
Scared, too late, to give you this, too late,

My love, my not-enough, perhaps-enough.

The Forest

At the edge of the wood moving in
This is trespass, crouch

For the pigeon's bolt, for the wren's alarm:
As though we were boys again.

Through silent halls of space moving outwards.
The sky is sagging, Autumn's weight took hold,

Like clouds full-charged with rottenness and gold:
We crept through the wire this morning

But I don't remember, through the laser heat of July
Or maybe September, the owls call to the owls,

A thought creeps through the grass:
Someone is out there.

The trees on every side march far away.
Follow them and one day you would come

Bearded and half-forgotten
On us again, and spy us through the trees,

Diminutive and lost, and stood at ease,
Each face upturned, the cold leaves pattering down.

Let us lay down our rifles and packs:
One day, perhaps, let this floor whirl up

In atom-swirls of discharge and of flux:
An Autumn wind to take us, torn apart,

And sift us through its roaring fission heart,
And leave us there, wherever that may be,

Like moths blown clear from cupped and gentling hands.

The Wound

It bristles like a moon beneath a telescope
And pleads like a child, but one gone bad
And meat-red. Like a polyp or a sponge
Is feeling feeling feeling, reaching out
For atom-motes in air
Which we can't see
But which must be there, which it draws into its mouth,
We think, with the undimmed brainless instinct for self-pleasure
Of milk-white creatures nestled on the deep
Of ocean plains, which we must eradicate
And scour, with sponges and with brushes made of wire,
Till the pictures we receive turn kitchen-white
And the groining taste of blood drains from our mouths.

A Breach

A breach, everywhere occurring, for someone
The sky ripped open, as was expected
And impossible. You will know what I mean.
Come back when you hear them say *dead*.

They want me to be humble, down to earth,
To write about the egg upon his beard.
But I see filmic rips, the day like breath
Rehealing over steamed-up glass that's nudged

But not before you've glimpsed a space beyond
And readjusted. Bright face who's gone,
This is natural as grass and wonderful
As roses. The world shakes like a heart
With every door-slam, exiting or start,
I touch it trembling until I follow.

Night Out

It's Friday night, so picture what you know,
The doors of every pub on every street
Like flute-stops flutter open and then close

And people—that is, crowds—I'm talking *Us*—
Pipe in and out like music improvised
By regimental bands gone mad, all brass

And boasting crotch—or, if you prefer,
The plug's been pulled on the world and now the lot
Is going down the drain in a swirl

Of End-of-Days excess—as usual.
Our faces lap and duplicate like coins
Tossed into water, floors of wishing wells,

And as the fingers of my mind trail through
The metal lags into reluctant furrows,
Frigid and shelving . . . get hence to the bar, you,

And bring me back a pint of Grolsch, some crisps,
And eighteen pints of Stella! A vodka coke,
Some gin—well get a pen and make a list—

A cider, whisky chaser, rum, and Guinness.
O towers of Babel blackness, capped with foam!
The world grows thick like dirty glass or mist

As the uninvited vision shambles through
Like a leant-on door which suddenly gives
And opens to a half-familiar room

That's half expected: ghosts mouthing at ghosts
And pawing at each other over tables
As I hurry through, exempt and lost,

And listen to the single voice that's rising
Like steam that breathes from off a crowd in winter.
'I am alive,' it says, 'alive and kicking,

But the words will not come out from me
When I'm awake—I'm a deaf man shouting,
A bell tolling through water, a hand on clay

Whose pressure's swallowed'—fingers now are plucking
At my sleeve—'lies spindle my tongue, custom
Enforces me, the sweet blind fucking

Of an animal is my stuttering in the dark'—
The voices dip into a low-pitched moan—
'In Britain we are cold or we're hysteric.'

I stumble out, half-choked, fighting off hands,
But even here a music strains and gutters
As if the sky's a flame exposed in gas

And I feel my mind bulge outward like a wall
Grown pregnant as it takes the wrecking ball
And gloves its impact. Almost against my will

The words come, telling a different story,
A nation blown to pieces on the Somme,
The purpose vested in ideas of glory

Blown to pieces, chemistry and machines
Tottering like infants over Europe—
The trees above me suddenly lean

Sideways, like gun dogs straining on a leash,
And a wind bowls in from every sky on earth.
I hunch and turn, listening to its rush

Across the landscape—dawn is very close now.
A few lonely figures are trailing home
And smoke is rising from kebab-van chimneys,

Woodcutters huts in a darkened forest.
Is this it? Letting myself go I whisper:
'We've always escaped, us people, lashed and pissed,

Or tried at least—it never really works.
There's a huge and graining instinct in us all,
Magnetic hub, migrating force in birds,

If we could only walk that path, could learn . . .'
On the way home I cross the bridge, look down:
Two swans are tucked asleep upon the river,

Riding the swan-road, necks tucked under wings,
Drifting away, twin baskets, perfect
As destiny. We have let ourselves dream.

What You Eat

1. Dining Out

What you do, do, we come from, go to
Dinner, *Impossible Honey,* the waiter said,
The name of the restaurant, tropical
Chandeliers nestled high
Amongst the guava, swollen and reared
Like the wrinkled balls of elephants,
But never fear, those carapace will crack
The guide, *M'butu*, says,
And give way to the blear
Of runny sweetness
You covetous so much,
Though they look from here
(He mused, his khakis rotten clear
To the inners of his thighs)
Like mines dropped down by the *Luftwaffe*,
Whose spiky touch sends boats straight down to hell,
Or skulls with jewels nailed through
Just for the hell of it,
Though the nails it seems, it's clear,
Are bees and obviously
At work or appear to be
From a distance, unaware of all the smoke,
The insurgence,
That you, *M'butu*, are shortly to send in.

2. English Breakfast

The 25 to Holborn, London, it's a commercial waste
Isn't it? or large parts of it,
Which we ride the bus through
To reach the oases people go to
On Upper Street and Soho
Where the thing won't be disturbed,
You know, that we do,
On a Sunday morning, hungover,
Hoxton and Borough,
To read the papers through our glasses
With a good old English breakfast
And a hand raised, I don't know,
In a *kingly* way,
That fashion, or manner, which makes it look as though
You were doing more than drinking a cappuccino.

3. On Your Plate

Bacon like a smile, and sausage too:
Beans like—just like red, or—I don't know,
The sweetness, their colour—
The egg, which is the main thing you order.
Laid out, the spread, which you turn
On its plate like I don't know,
An engineer, adjusting some wedge
Or vent or delicate nozzle
On a machine or some underfoot
Planetary geyser.

The Two Ages of a Footballer

I was rapid as a fish and hard to hold—
Between the midfield and back four
I danced and planted crops and mined for gold—
Had all the time I needed, sometimes more.

But now I cannot turn but feel a creak,
And do not dance but stand beyond the ball,
And watch the young ones mixing up their feet
And sometimes intervene, and sometimes score.

Identifying Trees

1.

Horse-chestnut candelabrum thrums the
Dusk not-dusk in summer not-quite-dusk—

O candelabrum! I am old-fashioned,
Passioned, stand with you

(A darker tree, remember one
Whose slow degrading certainty
We liked . . .)

2.

Always there and bigger, alder
Like the elder
Spurious brother I might have had
For the moment at least.
Switch all ways in the weather.

3.

Betula pendula, birchius, old gal:
I pity you as though you were
A nervous horse, its gaping roll-back
Of escaping eyes, the neck vein
Like a garaged turbo charger. But in secret,
Wow, to feel the generative electric
To such extent, intense, condensed
Reception of what is there, constantly.
Do women feel like this? Imagine so!

4.

Black Pine, Nereid's spread
Of hair in the Aegean, or Cornish seas

Of turquoise dropped in self-repeating skirls
Through sun-hacked blocks of water

To a bed as soft as linen, white
As powdered pearls.

5.

Fuzzy, tessellate, I call you
The Egyptian, initiate
Geometer of shapes I cannot see.
They make barrels from you, oaky
Barrels for whisky and beer.
But I think your leaves are like keys.

Sparrows

       —definitely
Sparrows, strung along or rather upon a wire that's strung
Outside your fourth floor bedroom window—
The blinds down, gone, the scene, just a sheen
Of fabricked light, uniform and
(One might almost say) a dream.

I lie awake with you asleep beside me.
Your lashes are the carpet on the perfect
Arabesque of this creation. Really,
I want to wake you! But instead
I imagine sparrows
Tumbling and squabbling like filmic Italians
Outside our fourth floor bedroom window
In a plot you need not know to understand:

Each push and gabble a rush of love,
Each fall defy all, simple, as we do.

O I Love You

O I love you pretty Annie
'Cos your face is passing fair
And your name it rhymes with . . . cranny,
And it has me in—despair.
How to write romantic poetry?
Fell in love without seeing her face.
Which only proves, she said, you can't efface
The fact you see just what you want to see.

But from the back, my God, the trace
Of down between her shoulder-blades,
The gap wherein the bra-strap's lace
Can leave a mark that's slow to fade—
Or quick, if rubbed. And this, she said, is lust
In action, evolution's fever,
Which you describe with words that sit like dust
Upon a combine engine's starting lever.

But still I'd trust, I say, the spark
That lives between us when we talk,
The fact that Noah's second ark
Would see us twinned in speech and thought.
Which means, she said, your promissory fuck
Comes backed with resources to make you friends,
So that, with kids and self-castrating pluck,
You'll learn to live off that when passion ends.

'Cos marriage, see, was made by men
To regulate the sexual pulse
And keep the beast within the pen
While we get on with something else.
Vapid face, love, goes out, candle and dark,

The world dispersing to an equal gloom:
You touch your way across a crowded room,
Touch doing what it needs to, and depart.

Conversation

I

You find a voice, this is it,
A tangential voice speaking
From a face that supposedly is
Yours, that supposedly is

II

An effigy beside you in the pub
Talking about dub
And politics, words
You hate to say and never think

III

What if a stranger were to find you where it is?
So lambent the conviction on its skin
They would take it for real, and you
A crack between the window and the bed

The Drum

In one photo she sits
On the lap of her partner, they smile
For the camera. The green drum,
Designed to carry oil,
Stands out from every shot.
It is still full, it thrums
With its contents.

Theresa Peggerty, former wife,
Told the jury of the strife
That kept inside her 'cos the drum
Would hang about the family home
With Mr Peggerty.
Mysteriously green, and full.

'I was always
Infuriated, there was so much
Rubbish around the yard,'
Ms Peggerty said,
'And everything.'
The barrel was just another thing,
Ms Peggerty says, should not have been
But always was.

'It was heavy.
I have touched it, I have tried
To handle it. My husband said
It was glue—it was green,
It stood in a corner. He said
It was glue, he said it had gone bad.'

Three Love Sonnets

I

O ballerina, rosa damascene,
We'll dance between the café and the bar,
And I will drape your hair with pilfered tinsel
And you will snap your stockings from afar—

Until the kettle boils, the kitchen steams,
The heat distills me . . . our new Ikea cups
Shepherd each breakfast: what faces, dear, what dreams
Propose themselves, guilty as mug shots?

But come to bed: turn over and your eyes
Will billow into mine, jumping from high.
If I can just maintain, if I recite
The story proper, avenues denied . . .
I wrap you round me like a blanket new-
Familiar as all blankets are.

II

God knows how, which is to say, I looked good
And so did you, and our conversation
Flirted sufficiently with evasion
To prove that neither one was *really* stupid.
And next, a courting that's as short as it is chaste,
And flattery as I pick up the bill
While you retreat strategically until
The rest of you's as naked as your face.

Is this, my dear, audition or transaction?
What other faces nudge between these thighs
To whisper *will you see this one again?*
We're fucking Proteus, and as I caliper this breast
I ask myself what pressures must be applied
To eradicate the memories of the rest.

III

We must turn to each other with guilt,
As though we'd sinned, and listen to the jungle
In our blood: vines cover your eyes, the split
Helices of umber fall, we are animal,
Cities go under and the temple of your thought
Is verdigrised with the moss that slicks the delta:
I was made to betray, as you will traitor me.

But pause: I see you're laughing from your armchair.
Do you remember that walk we made, at the flood?
A man had jumped in the river, to save
Someone, he had given himself away and emerged
Singing, himself completely, water jewelling his brow,
And as he walked away and left us you were whispering:
'This is love, and this is here, and this is now.'

A Kind of Love

As you came suddenly across to me
Upon your knees
Upon the sheets
I received your nuzzle into my throat
As if nothing could be more natural
Nothing so insubstantial
That you should love so hard you nip so close

But my hand upon your back had the wondering tenderness
Of someone handling equipment of which they are not sure
Which seems so delicate
But which, one suspects, might jump like a buzz-saw
If handled wrongly
Or the grain of the wood prove slovenly
And beyond all fathoming

Though the dream remains of shaping wood to steel
As it comes on
So the one is devoured beneath the other
Perfectly
Like water in the cogs of a mill's wheel

Chaos River Section

Chase and then chase the trace
Of ripple gone footloose
Through the water shedding space
Of the river, river,
Under and over,
The ripple in place like a gull
Setting into the storm,
Its yellow human eye.

The Summoning

You flit—the word is *ghosts*, but no,
We use that word—too slow, too slow—
A paleness, then, which is to say
Remove, the hand, whose every groove—
But no, no groove, but delicate
Proliferate of sub-
Cutaneous veins—
I lie—your squarish
Spot welder hands,
Blunter than mine,
I might be a pianist
You said—you said *an artist*—
Somewhere now at this,
The any-hour
Of witching, which is to say
Of living with a tracer pressed
To my heart
Like an ear upon a glass
To a wall in a dank hotel
You go, lovely down the tabletop
So slow, your hands unfolding
As if—you see?—disclosing
Coins, doves, palms, oh
Anything
To someone who is there.

Autumn-Time

The scuds and sops of leaves on streams
Like scrunched-up scraps of bread in bowls of soup—
Autumn coming. Autumn here
And back to school, the withdraw of the year,
As fishermen dink lines beyond themselves
And oaks collapse their spectrum, fade to red.

Waking Midwinter

The year is dying and the streets
Are never dark; the days are spare;
Waking alone I sleep alone
And dream a staircase carved from solid air.

There is no work. Down avenues of ice
I pass each day a kiss on encased leaves:
Slowly I'm learning ice is lived
In absence and uncertainties.

There was an aching in the space today
Between the trees, and disparate things
Now coalesce and move between
Themselves; that gutter and the bird who sings

Are grown the same; they circulate apart;
The melding of the air it is
That stings. Down avenues of ice
I pass each day an aching shape of kiss

That's not quite met. The face I long for
I fear: it struggles to reach me:
Today my watch broke, now I hear
Clock bells chiming, chime across the city.

'Can I create here . . .'

Can I create here, this little nook—
Is to remember—
Your head, your hair, like silk
Laid over warmth, the uncounterfeitable heat
On which you rode
Uniquely, crying at the train station—
But still you meet me—
Gone, now, I sit like the controller
In a room whose books and pencils, laptop, windows,
Comfort like dead switches
To a child in its game—
When I close my eyes—

This Civilisation

What's that look for, in you?
The psychopathic leer, as if you knew
Something I didn't: your eyeballs rung up
Like apples on a fruit machine,
But gone past their mark, leaving nothing but white.

Obsidian, marble, you seem to freeze:
And behind you, in the background,
The Mediterranean sea
Crawls and winks amongst itself,
Still skittish with the touch of
Alcibiades, Themistocles, Nelson:
It touches boats
And isolated rocks,
Shaking like an addict, still searching for its next
Quickened candidate:
                        It will find no-one,

Mad old lady, pigeon-struck crazy,
Giddy with our toxins and our gravied
Shit, its hormone mix
Of pillage, best ignored, let her go by,
The beggar.

                What's up with you?
Frozen like a gatepost
Or a statue, I could polish your eyes with my thumb:
Knocked over, drunk, you'd clump
Into sugary blocks,
A drug mule's betrayal of motive:
            Your colleagues stood back, aghast.

I can still hear the sea: fuming
Like an incense bowl swung high
Above the oxen led on ropes of flowers,
Marmoreal flesh and confident moos—
Worthy of a photograph or two.

Lift Off

      and the plane pulls clear
Like a lollipop from the mouth of a child
And the air does its mathematics on your head.
A trolley comes down; the air is squalid
With recycled gas; you eat something
And wish you hadn't. What films, do you think,
Will be shown? Outside

A mountainscape of thousand year old dreams
Assumes infinity in purest cloud.
Ziggurats and stacks and billowed towers
Bulge in pillowed landslides down crevasses
Where vapour clings and trances to the sides
That lack all direction. Here and there
The sun goes, roaming,
Touching points and edges
Like a creator in awe of its own creation,
Its ferocity, the pure indifference
Of a beauty

Which it realises, suddenly, is not its own,
That cannot be, a cold
Illegitimate spawning.

You wake inside to a stewardess coming through
With a happy face
And her family trailing behind her, down on the earth,
Like seaweed in the through-draught of the water,
Its chuckling braid.

Love hits like an explosion.

Levi

I wouldn't want to presume,
Levi, by dwelling on your battered pork-pie hat,
The one that makes you look, you think,
With a private and half-ironic glance
In the mirror of the rest-room, a bit like Jimmy Cagney
On the other side of the world;
Or on the slung-moon caffeine-pouches of your eyes,
Your penchant for saloon-bars
And coffee houses, the newspaper mastered
And perpetually under your arm, the taut and helpless
Prescience with which you enter the ghetto.
I wouldn't want, either,
For you to mourn for me
Were the tables to be reversed,
No individual sympathy: rather
To have you plunge like a muscled dolphin
Into the furious school of intelligence
That is purpose moving forward
Like a man from out the desert
Carrying words for all to read—
Honey of communality . . .

From the Sea Fields

At Nanjizal, by a brutal sea
I went to feel the spray and lions' heave
Heaving with a lion's tongue and sound of lions:

Watching from the heights as the sea came
Into the hollows of the bouldered shore,
Dark-throated, with the crested claws of the sun.

All roads lead here in this land.
All hills show the shock of blue,
The wild packs running beyond the granite palisades

And the old fields watching.
In pools at low tide the two are met
In tangle of reflected veins,

The one in the other.
These struts and spars of rusting kills
Are open hands, as delicate as flowers.

21st Century West

Each night, above my garden, your new comets
Chatter to each other on their way,
Asleep by their tail-lights, for touch-down by morning
And cocktails on the pavements of LA,

Delhi, Tokyo. Imperial officials
Sat, once, like this, counting wheat in their heads
In lonely desert towns,
Served with mint tea and focaccia bread,

Their eyes cased in black, little machines
For processing the world.
Noon, like a bored director, will cast them
As Gods, ivory palms and thighs of gold,

A logical progression, their skin
Faintly scented with the lusts
Performed on a red divan that morning,
Watched by the hotel's jaded parrots,

Aeschylus as a paunched figurine.
Later they will photograph the desert
And the sea, the endless sea
Of faces will produce a silver teapot.

Each night the comets pass above my head
And I imagine their landing,
It's beautiful, like nuclear blooms walking
Across the earth, on a dark computer screen.

His Grip

It requires the names, or so it seems to me:
Brabantazia and cowslip, hippuris
And tellumond. Garden-walking
Capture what I see,
Creamy beaks or cupcakes in serifs
That landslip from the trunk to which they cling.
Magnolia denudata, this is
Yulan or lily tree. Adamantine
Are my feet upon the ground, practical,
Because the multifoli -oed or -ate world
Could not exist sans cipher or a channel,
Sans cover, or control, or grip to hold
The axe-blade which I bring towards the pine.

Poem for a Country Pub

So, you'd sing of Chevy Chase and faerie queens?
With fiddle and bow
You'd boldly go
Back to how things might one day have been,

When people raised their music with their pint
And brought each day
Of frost and hay
To legendary order in the light

Of smouldering oaks which lit their fathers?
My friend, look up:
That loving cup
You lift is carried somewhere else by cameras

Which duplicate each song in black and white:
While metal carts
Drop sooty farts
To bring that pint of cider fresh with sulphite

From where it might have been to where you are.
Don't get me wrong—
I like your song—
But tell me, how's it go beyond this bar?

Export and infiltrate through what surrounds me?
Or play a game
Of switching names:
I'll be Friar Tuck and you be Thomas Hardy.

Adam's Curse

Grand amoeba knowing, know what I mean?
Goddamn *right* you do, you're a mother-fucking
Genius.
        As on one of those scientist's screens,
You know, those discs
On which the microscope suspends itself
And grips its tubing lens with one free fist
To frot away at the scene,
The activating jigger of those cells,
Laid out all clean and circumscribed
On the plate of their world
To fuck and kill and agitate, just like
              —o-ho!—
                      the mujahideen
Of scale! How they descend
And decimate the eye!
Such that I, by-and-by,
Begin to reconnoitre you askance
And wonder how I might take your head off
When you're not watching
        (Especially—my friend!—
        If you appear, as I am cogitating,
        To be planning on an outflank of some kind,
        Some kind of sating
        On the grazing herds of cunt which lie beyond
        Docile as mushrooms)
Much as the fellaheen, I imagine,
Observe the nomad organisation
Whose long-established cut of nature's bounty
Is passing out of fashion
Inversely to the swelling of my landlord's gut,
To the prick of the sword
And swinefever's ration.

This chromosome has come so far!
I toss it like a mother-fucking caber.

Playing

The next, the one I'll love, will smile
And her face unpeel like an apple
Maybe, to show you there,
Both unaware

Of what has happened.
O balding doll's head:
I can
Play as well as the next man.

Relationship in Two Parts

I

If I open my eyes
Outside the sun
Will sluice away from them

Like water from the deck of a tilting ship.
This morning you accused me
Of making too much toast.

I hung my head, guilty
Of your previous accusations.
Outside the sun is hoisted up

And burning hugely in a cold sky:
The bus wheezes and shuffles its feet,
Turns me this way and that

Like a bored photographer.
Silence in the kitchen, silence behind me:
Dim awareness of the morning light

Flaring in across the tabletop,
The two half-empty coffee cups,
The pot of jam translucently red

Like a jellied heart in glass.

II

I'll bring you out here, to where the cliffs
Pretend a lethal drop
But harbour little playrooms of themselves
Beneath the lip.
Scrambling down
The thrift and samphire shrug and dip,
Virgin to sight: possession

Of persistent love
Has brought them through the rip
And preoccupied whinny
Of the conquering wind.
I will not point out the lesson.
The boulders sleep like lichened seals.
The gleeful water ferries back and forth.

Co-ordinates

Six months left to live, they told me,
Quite certain. Quite, I said, from *quit*
And from *quittement*, completely.
Also, in bull-fighting, a move to distract

The bull with the fluttering cape.
Could I tell you anything you do not know?
In midsummer, a cricket ball thrown up
And going to take the catch, the field unmown.

'Beautiful, we barged . . .'

Beautiful, we barged upon, we barged, I was a barge upon
The tawny liquor sweetness of your body river,
My prow gone, the current
Like two hands upon a rope
That subsides-slinks, pulled down, gummed down with weed,
To vanish in the contact where the surface is,
The brink,
As rope dipped into acid will appear to drink
Elixir that erase it up to here—
The touch, no trace, obliterate embrace,
Though here the rope ploughs onward like a boat
Or snake gone into water, not afloat
But subaquatic now and lived remote
Forging as it's pulled, far-off and scoped
Only as a tremor in the river's throat.

Phwoar

Parchment-skinned and not flowing,
Your hair, any more, as Adonis
Or Morrison from *The Doors*:
As in a photo of mine (of yours, of my mother's)
Which a girlfriend idly picked up in the house
And, after surprise had lit out
Like a parrot's cry on waking
A thousand leagues from home,
She recognised my face-to-be in yours
Dad, but not as good looking—
And computing this, with a tilt inside her fingers,
Muttered with a mischief that I loved: *phwoar* . . .

Meadow Lane

Liam, walking back down Meadow Lane,
Having talked of narratives in prose
And film: how Orson Welles, you said, would earn

The resource for whatever masterpiece
He'd left unfinished in the open air—
A statue waiting with its lover's face

For feet and legs to put it standing there—
By taking any jobs that came his way,
Voiceovers and hosting gigs, the bare

Audacity of loss sustained each day
By two steaks, rare, and a pint of whisky, neat—
As we put down our pints of cider empty

And let our voices drift in bafflement
To blackened glass, beyond which we knew where
The lightless Isis leant its shelf of weight

Against the silver ribbon of the weir
And never seemed to move, though past that point
You know the river splits in springing clear

To nebulae of phosphorescent light
Which mark that place, like stars for navigation,
And send out sound, on calm untrafficked nights,

Traversing through the air in both directions
So that you'd meet it coming up or down
As though causality had been undone

And ran both ways—though tonight the wind
Has muddled any memories of it
So that, as I trace back and gather in

The twists and turns that lead up to this point,
I jump from where we split upon the bridge
And you turned left, and I continued right,

To end up here, half-sozzled, with a ridge
Of lamplight fissuring in summer rain,
Still miles from home and teetering on the edge

Of desolation, Liam, Meadow Lane
Empty, and everything as far from me
As nothing. But still, I would remain

A little longer here, detached and free—
Like a wound before the shock of wounding hits
Or an unearthed bolt of electricity—

Even if I had the child I don't
Waiting for me in a house called mine,
The child I never said I dreamt about

And held up in a field one summertime,
Its separate weight, its bright air-kicking squeals,
And felt the river in me surge and brim

And break its banks in a bright expanding wheel
To roll through everything. It might sound sweet,
I know, or pat, or merely laughable,

But cradling that familiar dreamy mite
I heard the sound of distant passing cars
And glimpsed how one day, tired and hurt, it might

Talk like Galileo with the stars.

Acknowledgements:

Acknowledgements are due to the editors of *Acumen, Ambit, Archipelago, Envoi, The London Magazine, nthposition, Pen Pusher, Poetry Ireland Review, PN Review, Poetry Review, Poetry Wales* and *The Reader*.